‍ W9-BXT-137

BLAST BACK!

THE CIVIL WAR

by Nancy Ohlin   illustrated by Adam Larkum

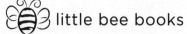

little bee books

CONTENTS

UNITED STATES
OF AMERICA
1861

Introduction

Have you ever heard people mention the Civil War and wonder what they were talking about? Did American states actually fight against other American states? Who won in the end? And what were they even fighting over to begin with?

Let's blast back in time for a little adventure and find out. . . .

A Brief History of the Civil War

You're wondering: What exactly *is* the Civil War?

A civil war is any war fought within a country between different groups of citizens. There have been many civil wars throughout history.

But when Americans talk about the "Civil War," they're talking specifically about the American Civil War that took place between 1861 and 1865.

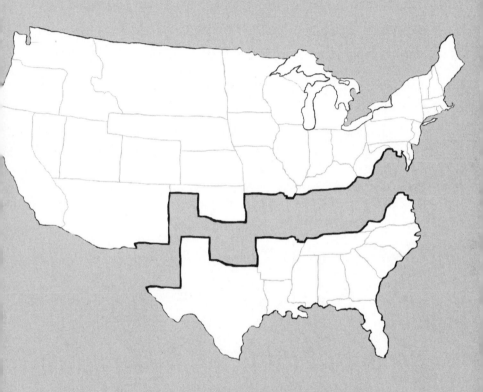

The American Civil War, which we will refer to as the Civil War from here on, was fought between the United States (the Union) and the Confederate States of America (the Confederacy). When the war began, the Union consisted of more than two dozen states and other lands in the Northeast, Midwest, Great Plains, and elsewhere. This side was also called the North, even though it wasn't limited to

the north geographically. The Confederate consisted of eleven Southern states that had seceded, or separated themselves, from the Union. This side was also called the South, and it lands *were* pretty much limited to the south geographically.

The Civil War is also known as the "War Between the States" and the "War of the Rebellion."

America before the Civil War

Before 1776, the United States was not its own country. Instead, it was a group of thirteen colonies that were under British rule. It was sometimes referred to as the United Colonies.

In 1775, the United Colonies went to war against Britain because they didn't like the way the British treated them. This war is known as the American Revolution. In 1776, a group of colonial representatives called the Continental Congress adopted a document that is commonly referred to as the Declaration of Independence. It declared that the colonies were no longer part of Britain but a separate country called the United States.

The last major battle of the American Revolution ended with the surrender of the British in Yorktown, Virginia, in October of 1781. In 1783, the British signed a peace treaty that recognized the United States as its own country. George Washington was elected as the first American president in 1789.

Over the following decades, the United States, or Union, expanded southward and westward, and new states and other lands were added. But with the growth of the country, tensions grew between the federal government and the individual states. Who was in charge of whom? Could states make their own laws, or did they have to abide by the federal laws? The North favored giving more power to the federal government. The South favored giving more power to the individual states.

At the heart of the disagreement was the issue of slavery.

The Thirteen Original Colonies

At the time of the American Revolution, the original colonies were Connecticut, Delaware, Georgia, Maryland, Massachusetts, New Hampshire, New Jersey, New York, North Carolina, Pennsylvania, Rhode Island, South Carolina, and Virginia.

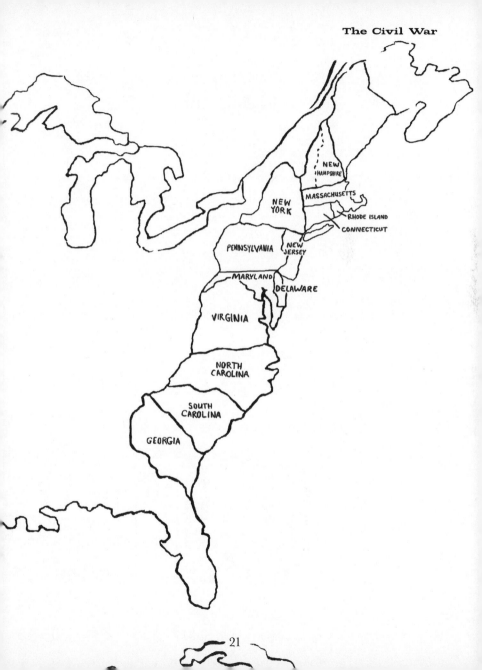

Statehood

Article IV, Section 3 of the US Constitution puts Congress in charge of admitting new states. (The Constitution is the most basic law in the country and has been in effect since 1788. Congress is the legislative, or lawmaking, part of the US government.)

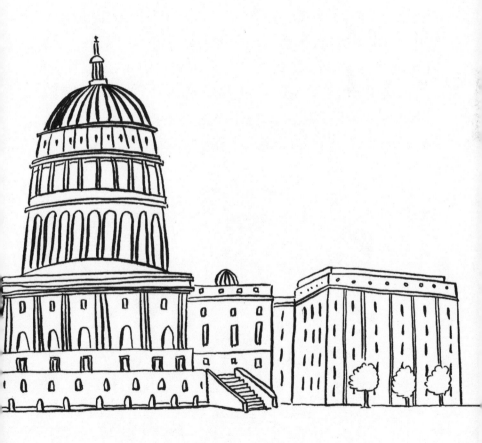

Slavery

There were slaves in America (and elsewhere) well before the Civil War. Beginning around the year 1500, black Africans were forced from their homes and taken to the New World to work for British, Dutch, and other European colonists. (The "New World" was a term used by Europeans to describe the Americas during this time.)

A slave was considered to be the legal property of another person and had to do whatever his or her owner wanted. Slaves had no freedom or rights. They were often separated from their families and forced to work under unbearably difficult conditions. Many were physically beaten or worse at the whim of their owners.

At the time of the American Revolution, all the colonies allowed slavery. But there was a great deal of antislavery sentiment, especially in the northern colonies. By 1804, the seven northernmost colonies, now states, had abolished, or gotten rid of, slavery. At this point, each state was allowed to decide if it wanted to be a "slave state," which permitted slavery, or a "free state," which didn't.

The Southern states were not happy about the growing antislavery sentiment in the country. Their economy was based on farms and plantations, and they wanted slaves to work them, especially as cotton production skyrocketed. The Northern states generally felt that slavery was morally wrong; furthermore, their economy was based on manufacturing, which used paid workers instead of slave labor.

By 1818, the Union had twenty-two states. Eleven were slave states and the other eleven were free states. Then Missouri applied to the US Congress to join the Union as new state—a new slave state. The Congress members from the free states weren't happy about that because the result would be twelve slave states and eleven free states. (This meant that the slave states would have more members—and power—in Congress.)

In 1819, Maine applied to join the Union as a free state. The following year, a deal called the Missouri Compromise was reached. Under this agreement, Missouri would be admitted as a slave state, and Maine would be admitted as a free state; however, there could be no slavery in future states or territories north of the southern border of Missouri. (Back then, a territory was an area in the United States that was not part of a state but had its own government.)

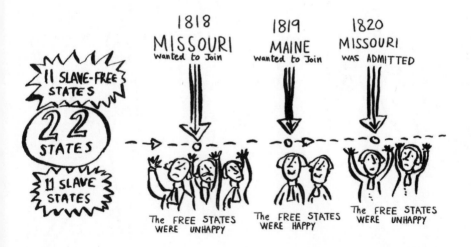

11 SLAVE-FREE STATES

22 STATES

11 SLAVE STATES

1818 MISSOURI Wanted to Join

1819 MAINE wanted to Join

1820 MISSOURI WAS ADMITTED

The FREE STATES WERE UNHAPPY

The FREE STATES WERE HAPPY

The FREE STATES WERE UNHAPPY

The Missouri Compromise lasted until 1854, when the Kansas–Nebraska Act was passed. This new act went against the Missouri Compromise because it allowed Kansas and Nebraska, which were north of the agreed-upon border, to join the Union as territories and to decide for themselves whether or not to allow slavery. There were violent protests over the passing of this act.

The tensions between the federal government and the individual states, and between the North and the South, continued to escalate over slavery.

More Cotton, More Slaves

In 1810, 178,000 bales of cotton were produced in the South. In 1860, this number jumped to 3,841,000 bales. In those fifty years, the number of slaves in America went from a little more than one million to almost four million.

The Dred Scott Case

In 1857, the Supreme Court, the highest court in the land, ruled on the case of Dred Scott. Scott had been the slave of a US Army officer in Missouri (a slave state). Scott moved with the officer to Illinois (a free state), then to Wisconsin (a free territory), and then back to Missouri, where the officer died.

After his death, Scott sued in court, saying that he was now a free man because he had lived on free soil for a time. The case went all the way up to the Supreme Court, which ruled against Scott; it also ruled that Congress could not make slavery illegal in territories and other areas that were not yet states.

The Underground Railroad

While some people were working hard to keep slavery legal, others were doing everything they could to make it *illegal* and to help slaves achieve their freedom.

A huge part of the antislavery movement was the Underground Railroad. For more than forty years before the start of the Civil War, this heroic effort helped slaves escape their bondage and find refuge.

The Underground Railroad was not a railroad at all; it was an organized network of homes and other safe havens where runaway slaves could hide while traveling to freedom. It extended through fourteen Northern states and up to British Canada. "Underground" referred to the fact that it was top secret. "Railroad" referred to the fact that train-related terms were used in order to make its activities even more secretive. "Lines" meant routes; "stations" meant the stopping places; "freight" meant the slaves; and "conductors" meant the people who sheltered the slaves.

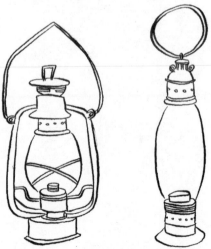

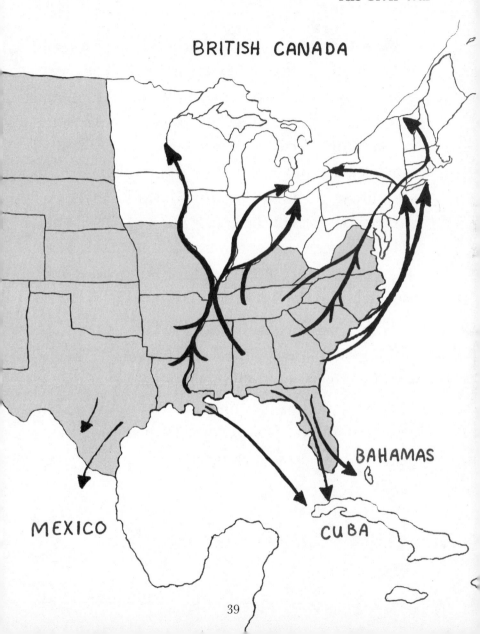

BRITISH CANADA

BAHAMAS

MEXICO

CUBA

With the Underground Railroad, a slave could run away from his or her owner and head north to the Canadian border, hiding in one station and then another. Once in Canada, that slave could not be returned to his or her owner or prosecuted (which meant put into jail or some other form of punishment). The Underground Railroad helped tens of thousands of slaves (the number is estimated to be between forty thousand and a hundred thousand) reach the Canadian border or at least find shelter in the Northern free states.

The Underground Railroad was run by abolitionists and other antislavery groups, including members of the Methodist, Quaker, and Mennonite religious communities. The Underground Railroad stopped their operations when the Civil War began.

The Fugitive Slave Acts

In 1793 and 1850, Congress passed a series of laws called the Fugitive Slave Acts. These laws made it illegal for slaves to run away from their owners or for anyone to help them do so.

The Abolition Movement

Abolitionists were people who wanted to abolish, or get rid of, slavery. Famous abolitionists include:

Harriet Tubman: Nicknamed the "Moses of her people," she was a former slave and a major figure in the Underground Railroad.

Sojourner Truth: A freed slave, she became a popular abolitionist speaker and was also a defender of women's rights.

John Brown: He was a white abolitionist who believed in violence as a way to fight against slavery. He was arrested, tried, and sentenced to death in 1859.

Frederick Douglass: He was an escaped slave who became one of the most important and dedicated civil rights leaders in the country. (Civil rights are the rights of citizens to have equality and freedom.) He oversaw the Underground Railroad movement in Rochester, New York.

Harriet Beecher Stowe: A white American author, she wrote an important antislavery novel called *Uncle Tom's Cabin* that was published in 1852.

Secession

Just as the thirteen original colonies seceded, or separated, from Britain and formed their own country, the South eventually did the same with the Union.

The Southern states had been threatening to secede from the Union for many years, especially over the issue of slavery. Things reached a critical point when Abraham Lincoln was elected president in 1860. President Lincoln was a member of the Republican Party, which had been formed in 1854. Republicans wanted to put major limits on the expansion of slavery. They wanted to keep new states that joined the Union from becoming slave states. Some Republicans wanted to outlaw slavery in every state of the Union.

The election of President Lincoln was the last straw for the South.

South Carolina made the first move. A special convention there voted to secede on December 20, 1860. Mississippi, Florida, Alabama, Georgia, and Louisiana followed in January and February of 1861. These six states formed a separate and independent government called the Confederate States of America, or the Confederacy, and elected Jefferson Davis to be their first president.

At this point, Lincoln had not been inaugurated, or sworn in, as president; President James Buchanan was still in charge. President Buchanan declared that the secession by the states was illegal, but he refused to send military troops to force the Confederate states back into the Union.

President Lincoln took office in March of 1861. Around the same time, Texas was admitted into the Confederacy. In his inauguration speech, President Lincoln tried to assure the South that he wouldn't interfere with their right to have slaves; he wanted to prevent a civil war and to restore the Union.

But his speech didn't work. A month later, war broke out.

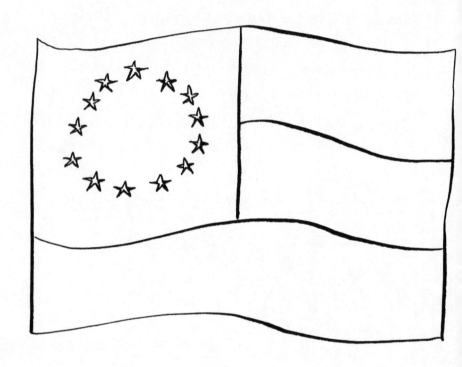

The Birth of the Confederacy

When the Southern states seceded and formed the Confederate States of America, they kept the same form of government as the Union, with a president and a Congress. They also kept the same Constitution (although they changed it to guarantee the institution of slavery).

The Confederates did create their own flag, though, and they adopted their own national anthem: "Dixie." They also printed their own currency based on a system of Confederate dollars. The paper bills were sometimes called "graybacks," just as Confederate soldiers were sometimes called "graybacks" because of the color of their uniforms.

The Beginning of the Civil War

On April 12, 1861, the Civil War began in Charleston, South Carolina.

Fort Sumter in Charleston was one of the two remaining military forts in a Confederate state that still belonged to the Union. When the Union commander there refused to give up control of the fort, Confederate troops took it by force.

Within a few days, the Union troops surrendered the fort. Both sides began to raise armies and prepare for more battles.

After the Battle of Fort Sumter, four more states seceded from the Union: Virginia, Arkansas, North Carolina, and Tennessee. The western part of Virginia decided to separate from the rest of the state instead of joining the Confederacy, though; this area later became the state of West Virginia. All the northernmost states stayed in the Union. So did Delaware, Maryland, Kentucky, and Missouri, even though they were "border states" that allowed slavery. (These states were located on the dividing line between the North and the South; their citizens were also divided on whether to side politically with the Union or Confederate.) Nebraska and what would later become North and South Dakota were also on the Union's side, even though they were not yet states at that time.

THE UNION

THE CONFEDERACY

Going into the war, the North seemed to have the advantage. They had more than two dozen states and territories and twenty-one million people; the South only had eleven states and nine million people, and nearly a quarter of them were slaves. The North also had more manufacturing plants, more railroads, more money, and better weapons production.

But the South had some advantages as well. They had a very long coastline that would be hard for the North to control or capture. They also had a strong military history and able leadership.

The Soldiers

After the surrender of Fort Sumter, President Lincoln called for seventy-five thousand Union troops to help stop the Confederate rebellion. But the rebellion continued on, and many more troops were needed on both sides.

For a while, both President Lincoln and President Davis relied on volunteers to step up and fight. But this did not provide enough soldiers. In 1862, the Confederate Congress approved a draft, which meant that the government could order men to join the military. The US Congress did the same in 1863. Many people in both the North and South were opposed to the drafts.

Soldiers were supposed to be between the ages of eighteen and forty-six. But there were exceptions. As the war wore on and many soldiers were injured or killed, both the Union and Confederacy recruited younger teens and older, even elderly, men.

Women were not allowed to fight, although some actually disguised themselves as men so they could be soldiers. Some women did this because they wanted to fight alongside their husbands, brothers, or other loved ones. Other women believed in the cause, just like the men. Women served in additional capacities as well, like nursing or spying.

Other groups were forbidden or discouraged from joining the army, like Native Americans and Mexican Americans. Some formed their own divisions and fought anyway. German, Italian, Jewish, and Irish immigrants, who also faced discrimination, did the same.

Neither free black men nor escaped slaves could join the Union military at first. But a few years into the war, new laws changed this, and many African Americans volunteered. They were not treated as well as the white soldiers. For example, they were paid less and could not become officers, and they were often given shabby uniforms and equipment. Still, they were willing to fight, and sixteen of them even won the Medal of Honor, the highest award for bravery in wartime.

Sergeant William Carney

Sergeant William Carney became the first African American soldier to receive the Medal of Honor. During the Battle of Fort Wagner in South Carolina, he was badly wounded but continued to lead his troops by crawling along the ground and holding the Union flag high.

Life in the Army

The average Civil War soldier spent very little time in combat. He spent most of his time in military camps, waiting for the next battle.

While he waited, he practiced drills, fixed equipment, and performed chores. He slept in tents, buildings called barracks, or in bivouac (which meant on the ground without a roof over his head). He ate his meals off tin plates and drank water or coffee. In his spare time, he might play cards, sing songs, or write letters back home. Many soldiers suffered from homesickness and loneliness.

Conditions in the military camps were harsh. As the war went on, many soldiers got sick or even died from measles, chicken pox, and other illnesses that were easily passed around in such close quarters. Soldiers also died from infections from battle wounds because there were no antibiotics (which are medicines used to fight infections). Unclean water and food shortages were serious problems too.

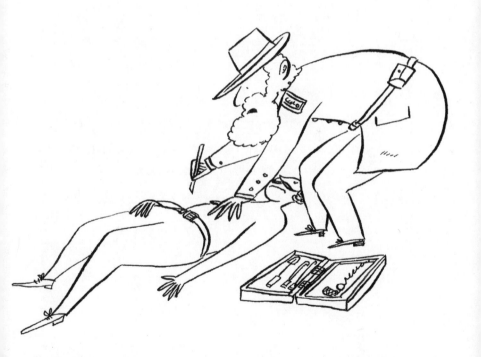

The Blue and the Gray

Union soldiers usually wore blue wool uniforms, and Confederate soldiers usually wore gray wool ones. During tough times, though, a Confederate soldier might have to scrape together a uniform made of light brown cloth that had been dyed with a crushed butternut dye. In fact, "Butternut" became a common nickname for a Confederate soldier.

Soldiers on both sides usually carried a knapsack or bag that might include a canteen for water, spare artillery, some food, extra clothes, and other personal items. They also carried weapons such as swords, rifles, and bayonets.

UNION   CONFEDERATE

How the War Was Fought

During the first year of the war, most of the battles took place in the border states. By the end of 1861, two major battlefronts emerged: in the East (particularly in Virginia, Maryland, and Pennsylvania) and in the West (starting with the Mississippi River and spreading from there). A major objective of both sides was to capture the other's capital: Washington, DC (the Union capital), and Richmond, Virginia (the Confederate capital).

Here is a timeline of important battles and other events, leading up to the end of the war in 1865:

- **July 1861:** The First Battle of Bull Run. Thirty thousand Union troops marched toward Richmond, Virginia. But Confederate troops blocked them at a stream called Bull Run and forced them back to Washington, DC. The Union was stunned by this defeat.

- **April 1862:** The Battle of Shiloh. In Tennessee, Confederate troops surprised General Ulysses S. Grant and his men at the Tennessee River. Fortunately for the Union, reinforcements arrived, and they managed to drive the Confederate troops away. Still, the casualties were disastrous; each side lost around ten thousand men.

- **August 1862:** The Second Battle of Bull Run. This cleared the way for Confederate troops to invade the North.

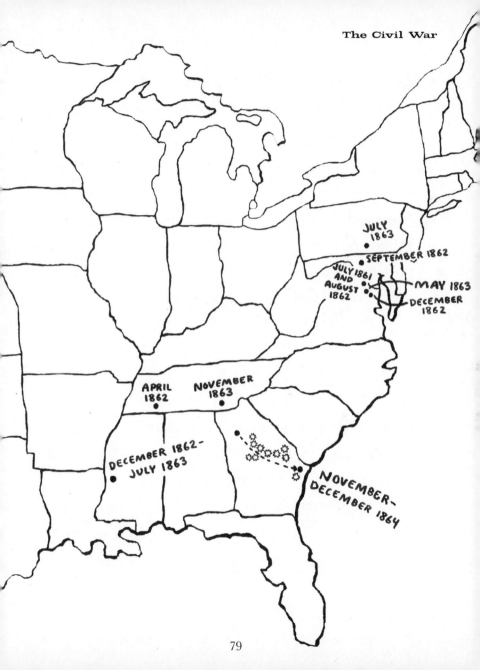

JULY 1863

SEPTEMBER 1862

JULY 1861 AND AUGUST 1862

MAY 1863

DECEMBER 1862

APRIL 1862

NOVEMBER 1863

DECEMBER 1862 - JULY 1863

NOVEMBER - DECEMBER 1864

- **September 1862:** The Battle of Antietam. The Union managed to stop the Confederates in Maryland.

- **December 1862:** The Battle of Fredericksburg. The Confederates won a dramatic victory in Virginia; the Union suffered more than twelve thousand casualties.

- **January 1863:** The Emancipation Proclamation. President Lincoln issued this proclamation, which promised freedom for slaves held in the Confederate states. This highlighted slavery as the main issue of the Civil War. It also paved the way for African Americans to finally join the US Army. Around one-hundred eighty thousand of them did so, which helped the Union troops greatly in terms of numbers.

- **May 1863:** The Battle of Chancellorsville. Confederate troops led by General Robert E. Lee defeated the Union troops in Virginia, then pushed north.

- **July 1863:** The Battle of Gettysburg. The Union crushed the Confederacy in Pennsylvania. This important victory turned things around for the Union.

- **December 1862 to July 1863:** The Vicksburg Campaign. This was a series of battles and maneuvers that centered on the Confederate fortress city of Vicksburg, Mississippi. Under General Grant, the Union troops finally captured it in July of 1863.

- **November 1863:** The Battle of Chattanooga. General Grant and General Sherman won this battle in Tennessee, even though the Confederates had claimed victory in the nearby Battle of Chickamauga Creek just two months earlier.

- **November and December 1864:** The March to the Sea. In September, General Sherman had captured Atlanta, Georgia, for the Union; this win paved the way for President Lincoln to get reelected. From Atlanta, General Sherman led his troops on the famous "March to the Sea" to the port town of Savannah. On their march, they destroyed supplies, railroads, and buildings, and spread terror among the civilians. In December, General Sherman and his men captured Savannah. The end of the war was near.

The Battle of the Monitor and Merrimack

The Civil War was fought on sea as well as on land. In March of 1862, there was a clash between two ironclad ships: the *Monitor*, a Union ship, and the *Merrimack*, which the Confederates renamed the *Virginia*. This battle, which was the first one ever between two ironclad battleships, showed that such ships were much better and stronger than the traditional wooden ones. New ironclad ships would have to be built immediately to replace the old wooden ones, which gave the North an advantage since they could build ships faster than the South.

The Gettysburg Address

Four months after the Battle of Gettysburg, the battlefield was dedicated as a national cemetery. At the ceremony, President Lincoln gave a speech that would come to be known as the "Gettysburg Address." In this now-famous speech, he honored the soldiers who had given their lives to make sure that everyone, including slaves, could be free. He also famously described democracy as a "government of the people, by the people, for the people."

More about Generals Grant, Sherman, Lee, and Jackson

Ulysses S. Grant: He began the war as a mere colonel and ended up in command of all the Union armies in 1864. In 1868, he was elected the eighteenth president of the United States.

William Tecumseh Sherman: Under Grant, Sherman was promoted to the position of major general in 1862. When Grant became president, he made Sherman the commanding general of the army.

Robert E. Lee: The son of a Revolutionary War hero, Lee left the US Army when his home state, Virginia, decided to join the Confederacy. Some consider him to be the Confederacy's greatest soldier.

Thomas "Stonewall" Jackson: Jackson earned his nickname because his brigade was like a "stone wall" against the Union troops in the First Battle of Bull Run.

Life in the North and South

For Northerners who were waiting at home, the first few years of the war were anxious times since the Union army was losing most of the battles. Still, the North managed to prosper and grow. The war created new jobs, as factories needed extra workers, including women, to make weapons and other equipment. Immigrants continued coming to the Northern cities and towns. The Union expanded as frontiersmen moved west to build new homes. As the North became larger and richer, its citizens had more time and money to enjoy leisure activities like reading books, going to plays, and watching (or playing) baseball games.

The South went in the opposite direction. Since the South was largely agricultural, they didn't have enough factories to produce necessary goods. With their men away at war, women and children were forced to do all the farm work and other chores. Food shortages were a problem, especially in the last years of the war. Also, since most of the battles were fought on Southern soil, Southern families feared for their safety in their own homes.

The End of the War

By the end of 1864 and the beginning of 1865, things were looking very bad for the Confederacy. Morale was low, and they were desperately short on both soldiers and supplies.

On April 3, 1865, General Grant and his men finally captured Richmond, the Confederate capital. He accepted General Lee's surrender on April 9 in a courthouse in Appomattox, Virginia.

But the Union suffered one more devastating defeat. On April 14, President Lincoln was shot and killed by a fanatical Confederate sympathizer named John Wilkes Booth. Booth thought that his action would boost the Confederacy's spirits and spur them to victory; he hadn't gotten the news of General Lee's surrender five days before, which had essentially ended the war.

Reconstruction

The period after the Civil War is called Reconstruction. Reconstruction had to do with the fate of the Southern states and how they might be rejoined with the Union.

Near the end of the war, President Lincoln had already been planning how to bring the Southern states back into the Union. After his death, his vice president, Andrew Johnson, became president. President Johnson wanted to continue with Lincoln's plan.

But this process was not easy. Many people in Congress disagreed with the plan. Some Congress members, called Radical Republicans, wanted to punish the South for what they had done before and during the war. When the Radical Republicans took control of Congress in 1867, they imposed military rule on the South, removed most of its leaders, and replaced them with white people from the North (whom the Southerners called "carpetbaggers") and African Americans.

In the meantime, nearly four million newly freed slaves were starting new lives. A government agency called the Freedmen's Bureau provided food, medical care, and schools for them. In July of 1868, the Fourteenth Amendment to the Constitution was passed, guaranteeing citizenship to African Americans. In February of 1870, the Fifteenth Amendment was passed, guaranteeing their right to vote. (However, it wasn't until the Voting Rights Act of 1965 that a majority of African Americans in the South were able to register to vote.)

By 1870, all eleven states of the former Confederacy had rejoined the Union. Reconstruction ended in 1877.

Whatever Happened to Jefferson Davis?

After the war, the former president of the Confederacy was charged with treason, but he never had a trial. He was sent to prison but released after two years.

The Legacy of the War

What was the legacy of the Civil War? What did it leave behind for later generations?

Besides ending the institution of slavery, the Civil War had other lasting impacts on the country. A very negative impact was the death toll. A staggering number of soldiers were lost in the war; recent estimates put the number at somewhere between seven hundred and fifty thousand and seven hundred and fifty thousand people, or around 2 percent of the US population in 1860.

The Civil War was also considered to be a transition between old-fashioned warfare and modern warfare. It was the first war in which submarines were used to sink warships; ironclad warships clashed with each other; the telegraph and railroad played important roles; and machine guns, land mines, and water mines were employed.

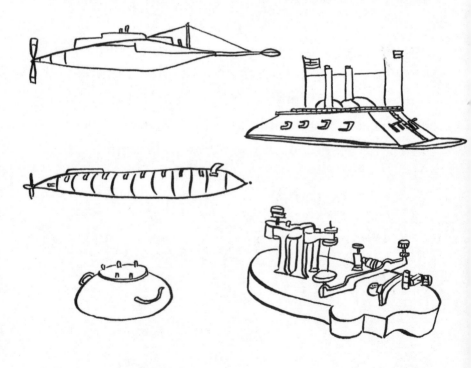

More tangible legacies of the war, like actual weapons and uniforms, can be found in Civil War museums such as the National Civil War Museum in Harrisburg, Pennsylvania. Many of the actual battlefields have been turned into parks and memorial sites that people can visit.

Well, it's been a great adventure.
Good-bye, Civil War!

Where to next?

Also available:

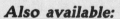

Coming in August 2016!

Selected Bibliography

Civil War Trust, www.civilwar.org

Encyclopedia Britannica Online, www.britannica.com

Encyclopedia Britannica Kids Online, www.kids.britannica.com

Eyewitness Civil War by John Stanchak, DK Publishing, 2000

The Library of Congress Civil War Desk Reference, edited by Margaret E. Wagner, Gary W. Gallagher, and Paul Finkelman, Simon and Schuster, 2002

National Archives and Records Administration, Compiled Service Records, Records of the Adjutant General's Office, 1780s–1917, RG 94, www.archives.gov

The Untold Civil War: Exploring the Human Side of War by James Robertson, National Geographic Books, 2011

NANCY OHLIN is the author of the YA novels *Always, Forever* and *Beauty* as well as the early chapter book series Greetings from Somewhere under the pseudonym Harper Paris. She lives in Ithaca, New York, with her husband, their two kids, two cats, a bunny, and assorted animals who happen to show up at their door. Visit her online at nancyohlin.com.

ADAM LARKUM is a freelance illustrator based in the United Kingdom. In his fifteen years of illustrating, he's worked on over forty books. In addition to his illustration work, he also dabbles in animation and develops characters for television.